Fashions of a
Decade
The 1940s

Fashions of a Decade

The 1940s

Patricia Baker

CHELSEA HOUSE
PUBLISHERS
An imprint of Infobase Publishing

Chelsea House
An imprint of Infobase Publishing
132 West 31st Street
New York NY 10001

Library of Congress Cataloging-in-Publication Data
Baker, Patricia.
Fashions of a decade. The 1940s/Patricia Baker
   p. cm.
   Includes bibliographical references and index
   ISBN 0-8160-6720-1 (alk. paper)
1. Clothing and dress—History—20th century—Juvenile literature. I. Title.
GT596.B32   2006
391.009/043—dc22   2006049934

Chelsea House books are available at special discounts when purchased in bulk quantities for businesses, associations, institutions, or sales promotions. Please call our Special Sales Department in New York at (212) 967-8800 or (800) 322-8755.

You can find Chelsea House on the World Wide Web at
http://www.chelseahouse.com

Author: Patricia Baker
Research for new edition: Kathy Elgin
Editor: Karen Taschek
Text design by Simon Borrough
Cover design by Dorothy M.Preston
Illustrations by Robert Price
Picture Research by Shelley Noronha

This new edition produced for Chelsea House by Bailey Publishing Associates Ltd.

Printed in China through Morris Press, Ltd.

MPI SB 10 9 8 7 6 5 4 3 2 1

This book is printed on acid-free paper.

Contents

Introduction 6

1 *V* for Victory 28

2 Paris Under Fire 32

3 The American Challenge 36

4 British Designers at War 40

5 Zoot-suiters, Spivs, and Zazous 44

6 Men at War and Peace 48

7 Hollywood 52

8 The New Look 56

Chronology 60

Glossary 62

Further Reading 63

Acknowledgments 63

Index 64

The 40s

Fashion wasn't exactly grabbing the headlines in the newspapers of 1940. As the decade began, the silhouette for both men and women was largely unchanged from the previous couple of years. The female shape consisted of wide, padded shoulders; a narrow natural waistline; thin hips; and a skirt that fell to just below the knee. For men also, the line fell in an inverted triangle from square shoulders down to the waist and hips. Heavy shoes provided a counterbalance in both cases.

Accessories were still essential for women. Hats remained popular, with styles varying from those tipped over the forehead to those planted firmly on the back of the head. During the war, however, hats were increasingly replaced by fabric head scarves and turbans, especially for women involved in war work in factories. It could be said that hats were one of the casualties of war. For a time, there was also a vogue for "snoods," a kind of pouch made of fabric or of knitted or crocheted yarn that held fashionable long hair in place at the nape of the neck.

Purses took the form of small box bags, especially in black plastic patent with a mirror in the lid. For daytime, women carried over-the-shoulder bags or large "clutch" bags without handles. "Crushed" suede gloves with flaring cuffs were popular for day wear. These were elbow length but were worn casually pushed down the arm; hence the name crushed. For evening wear, shirred (gathered with elastic thread) rayon jersey gloves were considered a glamour accessory around 1944 as fabric replaced leather.

Despite this continuity, there had already been occasional hints of change on the runways of the fashion salons in both Paris and New York, where a number of designers had been experimenting with a new silhouette focusing on the waist. For the moment, however, there were more serious things to worry about.

The World at War

The months of uncertainty and apprehension leading up to World War II were at last over; the real thing had begun. Europe was in bloody turmoil. Adolf Hitler's army had invaded Poland on September 1, 1939. Two days later, the British and French governments declared war on the German Third Reich. By the time the United States entered the conflict—following the Japanese attack on Pearl Harbor, Hawaii, on December 7, 1941—Norway, Denmark, Holland, Belgium, France, Yugoslavia, and Greece had fallen into Hitler's hands, and the European regions of the Soviet Union had only narrowly escaped the same fate.

It looked as if Britain's days were also numbered. Although the planes of the German Luftwaffe (air force) had been beaten off in the Battle of Britain (July–October, 1940), bombs continued to fall on the major British industrial cities and seaports, so that eight months later, one in every six families in London no longer had a home. Bombs weren't the only problem, however: it was

▼ Keeping them rolling. Like many others who suddenly found themselves in jobs previously reserved for men, this woman in uniform does her part on the Pennsylvania Railroad. Her passengers wear a fairly representative selection of wartime styles; the variety of different headgear worn by both sexes is particularly interesting.

▶ Many magazines, even those devoted to high fashion, began to give their articles and illustrative material a suitably patriotic wartime slant. However, the fur and velvet worn by the models in this shot from British *Vogue* in one of its 1942 high-fashion photo features must have seemed a far cry from the clothing worn by "real" women.

widely believed that chemical or gas warfare would be used against civilian populations, so gas masks were issued and carried by everyone. The fashionable London store Harvey Nichols advertised specially designed hooded gas-protection suits for women, "made of pure oiled silk … in dawn, apricot, rose, amethyst, eau-de-nil green, and pastel pink. The wearer can cover a distance of two hundred yards through mustard gas and the suit can be slipped over ordinary clothes in thirty-five seconds."

Rationing

All military personnel, on both sides of the Atlantic, had to be equipped with weapons and clothing, which meant that factories had to swing from producing consumer goods to war goods. The effects of this program were felt in Britain from 1941 and in North America from a little later. Everything seemed in short supply or about to be rationed. In Britain in 1943, even bathwater was limited to five inches in the tub, regardless of how many people shared the same water. Not surprisingly, the number of advertisements for deodorants suddenly increased!

▲Going out in the evening was difficult during wartime, especially in London and other large British cities where people had to dodge air raids. But when they did head for a dance hall, they expected something special, and the entertainers had to look their best. Here Benny Goodman and his orchestra perform in white tuxedo jackets, black ties and trousers, and red carnations.

▲The House of Chanel, founded in 1919, was a Paris landmark and was much missed during the 1940s in spite of Coco Chanel's personal unpopularity.

Chanel's War

Although designer Gabrielle "Coco" Chanel closed her Paris fashion house and disappeared from the fashion scene a year before the war started, her activities still caused controversy. In part, this was due to her relationship with a high Nazi official, but she was also a vocal supporter of the Vichy regime, despised by many French people and not recognized by the Allies. She regarded members of the French Resistance as criminals since they were breaking the terms of the armistice that France had arranged with the Germans. Because of this, Chanel had difficulty in reestablishing her salon, which did not reopen until 1954.

In Britain, clothes rationing started in earnest in June 1941. At first, adults received sixty-six coupons a year, but this was quickly reduced to forty-eight and then, by 1945, to thirty-six.

Extra coupons were available on the black market—the illegal trade in goods that were in short supply—and it was possible to buy some non-regulated fabric and garments. Supplies became increasingly limited, and prices were high, not only because of the scarcity, but also because a purchase tax was applied to such non-coupon items. Anyone caught trying to avoid the regulations faced a heavy fine. Lady Astor discovered this to her cost in 1943, after she had persuaded her American friends to send over clothes for her. She was fined 50 British pounds—ten times the cost of a lady's suit bought with coupons.

Not even the royal family was exempt from rationing. For her wedding to Philip Mountbatten (now the Duke of Edinburgh) in 1947, Princess Elizabeth was merely given an extra allowance, totaling 100 coupons. The government also specified that no "enemy" products were to be used for the wedding dress, which meant that British designer Norman Hartnell could use neither Japanese seed pearls nor Italian silk.

In the United States, restrictions and embargos were also having an effect. The ban on Japanese silk thread meant that nylon was replacing silk for stockings, but nylon itself was also required for military uses. The US Production Board issued Limitations Orders, such as the 1942 order L–85, which aimed to save 15 percent of domestic fabric production and 40 to 50 million pounds of wool and to freeze fashion, "thus forestalling any radical change … making existing clothes obsolete." The L-85 order specified the amount of fabric, pleat, and trimmings to be used as well as the length of jackets, skirts, and trouser legs and even the number of buttons. High heels were fixed at a maximum height of one inch in the United States, although the British government allowed a more generous two inches. Curiously, although the manufacture of metal zippers was for military use only, sequins were classified as unessential to the American war effort, and their supply and use were unrestricted.

▲ Because of clothing restrictions, many women had to abandon their dreams of a romantic wedding dress. Most couples, like this stylish pair married in 1940, managed a new suit and dress that could be worn again for Sunday best, and smartened up the overall effect with a flower corsage and a fashionable hat.

All the American clothing restrictions were lifted on VE (Victory in Europe) Day—May 8, 1945—when US price control chief, Chester Bowles, announced on the radio: "Now you can take your gasoline and fuel oil coupons and paste them in your memory book. Rationing has been lifted, too, on canned fruit and vegetables." With that, the orders for 187 million books of green-and-white ration coupons were canceled, but the price freeze that had been introduced in 1943 went on for another year. In Britain, rationing continued for three more painful years, until 1949, with some restrictions removed only in 1955.

Fashion in Wartime

With the German occupation of Paris in the summer of 1940, the fashion houses in Paris, under the leadership of Lucien Lelong, fought for survival and to protect their employees from being sent to enemy factories. They were no longer the second-largest exporting industry in France. For all intents and purposes, Paris

▲Wartime Utility fashions from Britain's Norman Hartnell, June 1943. Employing top designers was a clever way of making standardized designs more attractive, and ironically, it also meant that some women became better dressed as a result of wartime restrictions.

was totally cut off: suddenly, American and British designers were the trendsetters, with an important part to play in keeping public morale high. No longer designing solely for a small, exclusive clientele, their work was to encourage a positive response to the strict clothing regulations. In Britain, fashion designers, including many who had left France before the fall of Paris, came together in the Incorporated Society of London Fashion Designers (ISLFD), working with the government's Board of Trade. Similarly, designers in the United States involved themselves in the war effort, either directly—as in the case of Mainbocher, who designed the WAVES (Women Accepted for Voluntary Emergency Service) uniform—or working within the government stipulations laid out in the L-85 order. American fashion journalists, facing life without Paris, suddenly realized the talent on their own doorsteps, and American fashion houses began to receive the recognition they richly deserved. It was a short-lived but sweet triumph.

For the average person, of course, Hollywood films offered the usual fashion inspiration, although costume designers had to work within the same fabric restrictions as everybody else. The government made frequent appeals to designers and stars to help the war effort by promoting various styles.

To play their part in the war effort, ordinary women were told: "Use it up, wear it out, make it do, or do without." They became increasingly adept at making do, taking garments apart and restyling them. The media constantly offered advice and hints, such as how to make coats out of old blankets. In New York City, there was a drive for old furs that were then made into fur-lined vests for the merchant marine.

▲Ann Sheridan, the "oomph girl" or "sweater girl" used knitwear to show off her ample curves.

Sweaters—a Health Hazard?

One of the most popular garments of the 1940s was the sweater, but at the Vought-Sikorsky Aircraft Corporation in America, fifty-three women were sent home for wearing them. At first, management explained that the ban was on moral grounds: sweaters were too sexy. But when the union pointed out that sweaters were considered suitable for office workers, the company cited safety reasons. The National Safety Council confirmed that sweaters might easily catch fire because they attracted static electricity, and if caught in machinery, they would not rip and so might pull the wearer in too. Hollywood's Ann Sheridan, known as the "Oomph girl," joined the dispute and said that sweaters themselves weren't bad, but a little girl in a big sweater might be a safety hazard, while a big girl in a small sweater might be a moral one. Finally the Conciliation Service of the US Labor Department had to intervene.

▲Sweethearts of the Forces! Contestants from the various women's armed services gather in New York to compete for the title of "Service Cover Girl of 1944."

▲ As women rediscovered a talent for home dressmaking, publications obliged with cheap patterns and style suggestions.

A War Diet

The new year in 1940 was marked in Britain by the introduction of food rationing. Each adult was allowed twelve ounces of sugar, four ounces of butter, and four ounces of bacon or ham every week. By the end of that summer, one pound of meat per person was permitted, but the butter ration had been halved, and the restrictions were soon extended to include tea and cheese. Eggs, too, were strictly rationed: one advertisement in a local paper ran "Wanted: egg timer, sentimental reasons. Wanted: egg, same reason." Not only did the end of the war bring no immediate relief, but bread rationing was introduced and the basic food allowance was further cut, so that by 1948, the average person was worse off than during the war.

Rationing for the Parisians under Nazi occupation began in September 1940. Each adult was allowed twelve ounces of bread a day but only about five ounces of meat and cheese for a whole month. Sugar and coffee were like gold dust. Within six months, rice, noodles, fats (including soaps), fish, tobacco, textiles, and wine were all rationed. By December 1944, fuel was in such short supply that cooking was permitted for only one to two hours at lunchtime and an hour in the evening. It was another four-and-a-half years before rationing was lifted.

The weekly rations for a British family in wartime look very meager to our eyes.

"Margo"

"Yvonne"

"Jeanne"

"MARGO"
Exquisitely tailored Frock, intricate detail on bodice, pleats front of skirt. In pastel shades of blue, green, rose and beige. Sizes 38, 40, 42 and 44 in. **£9.11.2**
(11 coupons)

Model Gowns
FIRST FLOOR

"YVONNE"
Attractive Frock, cowl neck, jumper effect, unusual V design on bodice and pocket. In pastel shades of blue, green, rose and beige. Sizes 38, 40, 42 and 44 in.
(11 coupons) **£9.2.5**

"JEANNE"
Extremely neat Jumper Suit, shirt collar and buttoned-through front, insets on bodice. In pastel shades of blue, green, rose and beige. Sizes 38, 40, 42 and 44 in.
(14 coupons) **£10.18.11**

◄ Non-Utility clothes in wartime Britain often followed the styles of the official Utility designers and many displayed the slightly military influence in tunic-style tailoring.

►Advertisers never passed up a chance to cash in on the theme of the moment. Here, in February 1945, the fashionably patriotic appeal of servicemen is harnessed to promote the sale of coffee. Note how the waitress has her hair tied back in a style similar to that suggested for factory work.

"Got any Gum, Chum?"

With the United States entering the war in 1942, increasing numbers of American servicemen were stationed in Britain before being moved to the battlefront. It quickly became apparent that although they shared the same language, the two cultures were very different and both governments offered advice on codes of behavior. The American GI was advised: "Don't comment on politics. Don't try to tell the British that America won the last war. NEVER criticize the King or Queen. Don't criticize food, beer, or cigarettes.... Use your head before you sound off, and remember how long the British alone have held Hitler off. If the British look dowdy and badly dressed it is not because they do not like good clothes or know how to wear them. All clothes are rationed. Old clothes are good form."

The British newspapers in turn asked their readers to remember that the Americans "are foreigners ... and that the mistakes they make are likely to spring from too quick enthusiasm and too little background; that though we may be spiritually far more civilized, materially they have the advantage."

With so many men on both sides of the Atlantic drafted into military service, it was up to women to ease the very real shortage of labor, both on the farms and in the factories. Quickly, the traditional barriers defining "men's work" and "women's work" collapsed, along with the social conventions relating to dressing up for certain activities. Jeans and other pants and one-piece coveralls were now socially acceptable as women's wear at work, while scarce supplies combined with safety regulations to dictate new hairstyles. Although differences in wages remained for some time, many women enjoyed the greater opportunities that war work offered. They were now expected to play a full and active role in society, and this was reflected in the romantic fiction and films of the time. In hits like *His Girl Friday* (1940), the square-shouldered, short-skirted heroine was portrayed as working toward self-fulfillment—and finding the man of her dreams along the way. There was no hint that to keep him, she was expected to give up her quest.

WHEN HOSPITALITY'S IN THE AIR...

IT'S MAXWELL HOUSE COFFEE TIME!

There's good cheer and a warm welcome in every cup of this richer, finer coffee!

A Product of General Foods

● Whether it's open house for scores of service men . . . or a quiet evening at home with a friend or two . . . hospitality time is Maxwell House Coffee Time! This famous coffee, bought and enjoyed by more people than any other brand in the world, adds a gracious note of welcome and friendly good cheer to any occasion.

Fine Latin-American coffees are skillfully blended to bring you—in Maxwell House—a coffee you'll *completely* enjoy, and be proud to serve your guests. Manizales coffees for mellowness . . . Bucaramangas for full body . . . Medellins for rich flavor . . . Central and South American coffees for vigor. Then Radiant Roasting develops the *full* flavor of every coffee bean in this famous blend. In victory bag or vacuum jar, Maxwell House Coffee is truly "Good to the Last Drop!"

Good to the last drop!

◀ For the youngsters in the ideal American family, casual style meant bobby sox, plaid skirts, and linen jackets with the characteristic wide shoulders of the period. The well-appointed kitchen, including the latest model of refrigerator, indicates that this family is quite well off.

▼Newly liberated ex-servicemen stride out in their "demob suits." Although there were complaints about the lack of choice and poor quality of the fabric, most men were glad to be finally out of uniform, and had never been particularly fashion conscious anyway.

▲Chinese and American combat pilots, about to embark on a mission, are wearing the war's most influential garment, the sheepskin jacket.

Only Angels Have Wings

For many, the wartime pilot was the hero of the hour, especially after the Battle of Britain. As Gary Cooper showed in *For Whom the Bell Tolls* (1943), the pilot was the twentieth-century version of the medieval knight with his protective clothing going forth alone or with a few friends to vanquish the enemy and put the world to rights. His heavy sheepskin jacket—called the Shearling among American airmen and the Irvin in Royal Air Force circles—set him apart from the men of the other services. Everyone wanted to be identified with the image. Even Anglo-American designer Charles James claimed his prewar heavily quilted ladies' jacket, made of Chinese silk, was the inspiration behind the World War II Shearling United States Air Force jacket.

Winning the Peace

The end of the war brought its own problems. The process of demobilization released millions of men from military service, and finding work for them was an urgent priority. Suddenly, the women workers were no longer needed. Governments began a crash program to persuade them that their place, happiness, and future were in the home, while the men themselves had to readjust to home life and the realization that in their absence, the women had managed quite well without them.

On leaving military service, each man was discharged in his service uniform, given a $50 clothing allowance that included a suit, shirt, tie, socks, hat, and a pair of shoes—and sent on his way. Menswear did not undergo any radical change from the prewar to the postwar era. This may have been because the tailors and manufacturers, after half a decade of war, weren't able to make anything other than a suit based on late thirties styling. It's also possible that men themselves, already insecure in their new civilian lives, preferred this conservative look, which had almost a military conformity about it. There were a couple of exceptions. The zoot-suiters and spivs reveled in their exaggerated style of dress, but the general public disapproved of such displays, and in Britain in particular, it was associated with the seamy side of life and racketeering.

▲Again, advertising catches the spirit of the moment: the typical American family is busily sweeping away memories of austerity with some postwar spring cleaning. Top-Siders (worn by the young man in the foreground), shorts, and sleeveless sweaters sum up the American casual look, linked here with the growing thirst for Coca Cola.

◄ As these post-war sketches show, a return to longer, fuller styles followed on from the restraints of wartime conditions

▲ All the news that's fit to print. The ultra-brief bikini swimsuit makes its entrance in summer 1946, complete with newsprint motifs.

Baring the Midriff

The US government should be thanked for the introduction of the two-piece bathing suit. In 1943, it ordered that the fabric used in women's swimwear was to be reduced by one-tenth as part of its policy to reduce textile waste. The little "skirt" panel of the one-piece was the first victim of the cuts, and then the one-piece itself was attacked. The two-piece, and the midriff, were born. Three years later, American nuclear tests carried out on Bikini Atoll in the South Pacific inspired the little-known Parisian designer Louis Rear to name his latest swimwear design the "bikini." He said later that this was because the name symbolized "The Ultimate." In a similar way, the incredible power of the atomic bomb, as demonstrated at Hiroshima in 1945, led to a rash of "atomic" products, such as Atomic dry cleaners, Atomic hair restorer, and even Atomic pudding.

▲Elbow-length capes and full-length leather gloves are key elements of New Look outdoor wear for 1948. Dior's bombshell shattered the complacency of designers hoping to revert to safe, late-1930s styles.

In the United States, rationing and restrictions were quickly lifted, and the country moved speedily from full-scale armaments manufacture into mass domestic production, enjoying the increased prosperity that war work had brought for many. In Europe and Britain, however, the process took much longer. The war had destroyed not only factories and houses, but also ports and rail yards. National economies were in serious trouble, and Britain itself was virtually bankrupt. Rationing continued and was even more rigorously applied.

Enter Monsieur Dior

To many in France and abroad, the fact that the fashion houses continued to operate during the war smacked of collaboration with the Nazis. Matters were made worse when, after liberation, pictures of the Paris collections were seen abroad. Garment after garment seemed to ignore the restrictions and regulations that had bound designers in Britain and the United States. And when Christian Dior unveiled his "Corolla" (flower-like) collection in 1947—quickly named the New Look—postwar murmurs about past collaboration erupted into roars of disapproval. Government officials in London and Washington took one look at the amount of fabric used in the Dior dresses and warned that the newly revived postwar economies could be fatally damaged if such extravagance were copied.

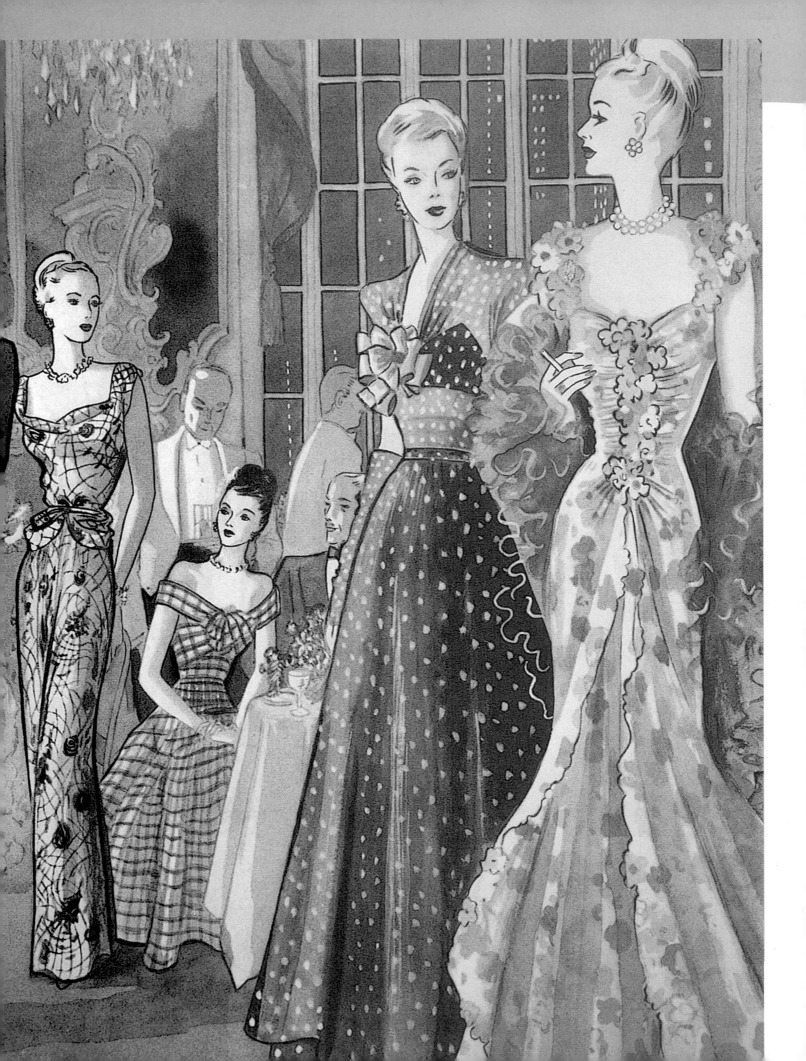

▲Dramatic stripes and decorative gathers lend excitement to the latest stretch swimsuits from Jantzen, 1948.

▶Rainwear for the man about town: Austin Reed of London's version of the man's overcoat, trilby hat, umbrella, and kid gloves. Broad-shouldered styles like these were widely popular in the postwar forties.

◀For the first few years after the war, there was uncertainty about the direction fashion was to take. Some American designers responded with designs of great luxury and femininity, like these 1946 evening dresses from (left to right) Hattie Carnegie, Adele Simpson, Nettie Rosenstein, and Muriel King. The appearance of full skirts and narrow waists foreshadows the coming of the New Look in 1947.

A Barbaric New Era?

Only in the last years of the war did the true scale of its horror begin to be realized. With the Allied advance into Europe, the reality of the Nazi concentration camps was uncovered. The news and the horrifying pictures stunned everyone. It seemed impossible that humans could inflict such cruelty on others. Almost 6 million people died in what is now called the Holocaust. Prisoners of war returning from Japanese camps showed that inhumanity was not confined to Europe, and as the atrocities suffered by hundreds of thousands of Chinese showed, was not inflicted just on Europeans. In early August 1945, the atomic bombs dropped by America on Hiroshima and then Nagasaki unleashed a monstrous new power of destruction.

Dior, however, had timed it perfectly. Women on both sides of the Atlantic were eager for change. They had had enough of square shoulders, short skirts, and dark colors. It all looked so military, so functional—so dull. They fell for Dior's curvaceous line, which accentuated the bust, the waist, the hips, and the ankles, and the sheer extravagance of yards and yards of fabric.

Perhaps the wartime fashion designers had done their job too well. From serving a small élite clientele, they now enjoyed enormous public prestige and influence over a much wider section of society. Whereas in the 1930s, fashion had had little immediate or direct impact on the general public, now cheap mass production—the result of reorganization to meet war demand—meant that everyone could have copies of model designs quickly and at a fraction of the original cost. Although the fashion houses still relied on their established clientele, their fate was increasingly decided by fashion journalists, who gave a thumbs-up or thumbs-down on the collections. To get cash flowing into the fashion house and increase publicity—and sometimes to offset hostile criticism of a collection—the designer's name was used to sell everything from scarves to underwear and perfume. By the end of the decade, the fashion houses had begun to play the "name game," promoting the cult of the individual designer.

▲The wasp-waist demanded by the New Look was not achieved without effort, as we can see from this shot of models lacing each other into tight corsets. At home, presumably, husbands were pressed into service.

▶New Look in New York. The "outrageous" Christian Dior arrives by sea to promote his designs in the United States in April 1948.

►A glamorous 1947 evening dress by America's Norman Norell, featuring a full white chiffon skirt with a daringly low-cut, halter-neck leopard-print bodice. The New Look shape can be seen in the nipped waist and accentuated hips.

◄ The war proved a spur to developments in many areas of material technology from which fashion was to benefit. This new range of rainwear from B. F. Goodrich was made from a new waterproof fabric called Koroseal.

▼The postwar passion for new technology was swiftly spreading to cars. As we can see, the advertising for the smart 1949 Oldsmobile went beyond "new look" to "Futuramics" and included terms like "rocket engine." The sleek lines of the Oldsmobile look forward to the streamlined styling of the 1950s.

The film that's be than a duck's back—

bial duck's back is a pared to *Koroseal* film; a shower, and it's dry it it can't absorb any water. t's easy to keep new and g—dirt doesn't penetrate, s easy. So—raincoats don't can even be folded away stick nor crack. And as le of a *Koroseal* film or sheet, n't penetrate—they are ideal oats as well as raincoats. flexible synthetic has a hun-

be washed almost as easily as glass. Garden hose doesn't need to be pampered—leave it out in sun or winter (and it's ⅓ lighter, too). Baby pants are clean with a slosh in soapy water. Shower curtains never peel, never become brittle or paperlike.

Why?

Koroseal flexible synthetic was developed by B. F. Goodrich from limestone, coke and salt. No rubber to be attacked by air, no odor, no pores to

Made of toug itself is tough— and many in outwears o' times over.

Koroseal any col gree c soft, or ri

NEW "Holiday" COUPÉ

THE SATURDAY EVENING POST

Hold fast to your heart when you meet this one! You'll see the most dramatic of Oldsmobile's Futuramics— the smartest looking car on the road—the Holiday Coupé. Look at those lines . . . low, lovely and luxurious—a new basis for beauty in motor cars! But it's not only the ultra-advanced design—the superb sweep of the flowing Futuramic lines that distinguish this beautiful car. For this is a "Rocket" Engine car—more active than your imagination—free and fleet and so vibrantly alive that you can't believe it until you try it! So for the finest "Holiday" you've ever known, see and drive the newest Futuramic—Oldsmobile's Holiday Coupé!

FUTURAMIC OLDSM

◄ With their bobby sox and pennyloafers, pleated skirts, sweaters, round collars, and tied back hair, these girls look young for their age, but they are wearing the "uniform" of the average twelve- to seventeen-year-old. But don't call them teenagers: the term was not invented until the 1950s.

The Bobby Sox Idol

The format orchestration of the big band was losing its appeal in favor of a new "intimacy" with radio listeners as Bing Crosby showed what complete mastery of the microphone could achieve. As Bing crooned his way into the dreams of adult women on both sides of the Atlantic, Frank Sinatra became the idol of teenage girls—the "Sultan of Swoon," as his press agent put it. He had started work singing for the big bands, where he learned, as he said, to "play" his voice just like musicians played their instruments, and his artistry in phrasing a song never deserted him. He explained his immense success in the early 1940s by saying: "It was the war years, and there was great loneliness. I was the boy in every corner drugstore who'd gone off, drafted to the war. That was all."

▲Frank Sinatra, king of the crooners, was always cool in wide lapels, top-pleat trousers, and big cufflinks.

To the Ladies

These gallant young women are dedicated to the service of our country. WAVE, WAC, SPAR, Marine, Cadet Nurse—they know that every ounce of work and loyalty is urgently needed now. They and millions of other Americans are putting all their hearts and energies into the fight for Victory. To them, Canada Dry, "the Champagne of Ginger Ales," an old family friend, says: Keep up the good work!

Just as soon as conditions permit, we hope to be able to fully meet the ever-increasing demand for Canada Dry Ginger Ale...and again make "The Champagne of Ginger Ales" available to you in the handy 5¢ individual bottle.

SO DELICIOUS, SO PURE, SO REFRESHING . . . ENJOYED THE WORLD OVER!

CANADA WORLD FAMOUS DRY

"The Champagne of Ginger Ales"

◄ Wartime advertising saluted the role of women in the armed forces, associating their contribution with social activities (left). In the postwar period, women regained their femininity but were hard pressed to hold on to their newfound independence.

► In essence, the look of the late forties was conservative and understated: the still essential accessories of hat and gloves complete an outfit of tweed day wear that might be worn for a visit to town.

V for Victory

War Work

As the factories moved into munitions and other war production, consumer goods became scarce, and rationing was the only fair way of distributing limited supplies to everyone. Some raw materials were completely unavailable and sacrifices had to be made, while general shortages led to some ingenious solutions.

The US L-85 order was geared to save 15 percent of domestic fabric production by banning such items as full skirts and knife pleats. Cuffs, double yokes, patch pockets, and attached hoods were all banned as part of a general "no fabric on fabric" rule. Order M-217 conserved leather and limited shoes to six colors, while laces and some kinds of embroidery were restricted by order L-116.

The need to save 10 percent of the fabric in women's bathing suits led to the happy invention of the two-piece suit. As the *Wall Street Journal* reported: "The saving has been effected—in the region of the midriff. The two-piece bathing suit now is tied in with the war as closely as the zipperless dress and the pleatless skirt."

Given the widespread difficulties in obtaining entire new wardrobes, accessories such as hats, gloves, and handbags became very important. Dickeys—or collars, some with extended shirtfronts—were often worn beneath sweaters instead of a blouse, as were jabots, often in the form of a standing band collar with an attached ruffle at the front.

SNACK FOR A WAAC

It's a lively life in the Army . . . and the delicious lift of a Milky Way is welcomed often. Milky Ways renew energy quickly . . . and every bite tastes so good. First you put your teeth into a thick coating of pure milk chocolate . . . then a layer of smooth creamy caramel . . . and in the center, luscious chocolate nougat, richly flavored with real malted milk. No other candy has the special deliciousness of a Milky Way!

▲Even chocolate candy bars got the patriotic treatment and were advertised as part of the US war effort.

►Nylons, already just a happy memory for British women, were fast disappearing from the stores in America too.

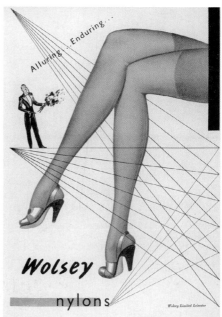

Alluring . . . Enduring . . .

Wolsey
nylons

Designed for War

American dress manufacturers had to design their styles to be worn without girdles since the use of rubber in girdles was banned. One dress manufacturer advertised: "No girdle required for this dress … with no fastenings (zippers gone to war) adjustable at waist and bust." Another ad read: "Duration suit: both jacket and skirt … are adjustable at the waistline; designed for wear with or without a girdle."

While some corset manufacturers designed rubberless girdles—one even went back to using whalebone—women were being advised to adjust to life without their

◄ In one of the most famous rallying posters of the period, "Rosie the Riveter" persuaded thousands of women to volunteer for work in factories or heavy industry. They found themselves doing work they had never dreamed themselves capable of and enjoying it.

►The military braid hairstyle, approved for women in wartime. The curls were intended to retain some measure of femininity in what was essentially a rather severe style.

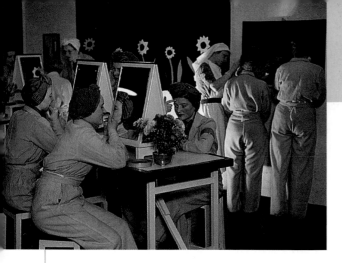

◄ Coveralls and head scarves meant that hairstyles were irrelevant to these ordnance factory workers, at least during working hours.

► Slacks, blouse and jacket, and flat-heeled shoes: a practical look for the working woman.

restraining help. *McCall's* Washington newsletter warned: "Just what the lack of girdles will eventually do to styles is anyone's guess, but Washington's experts don't hold out much hope for a return to solid, hefty bulges."

With increasing numbers of women drawn into war work, safety made its own demands, and companies encouraged their designers to promote safe, attractive outfits. Vera Maxwell, for example, created the coveralls for women working for Sperry Gyroscope. *McCall's* in 1942 listed the advantages in work wear: "The girl in the defense factory really has all the luck. She wears a coverall for work and thereby saves clothes, time, money, and nervous energy. And look at all the nice green cash she picks out of the envelope each week!"

Women were urged to have their hair cut short in the new "vingle" (a close-cropped haircut), the victory roll, or the liberty cut, which needed to be cut only once every three months. This served more than one purpose: hairpins were unavailable, hats needed coupons, and women in wartime factories were being badly injured as a result of getting their hair caught in machinery. The immensely popular "peekaboo" hairstyle worn by American movie star Veronica Lake, with its cascade of hair over one eye, was now considered hazardous. When appealed to, Veronica Lake patriotically, and very publicly, changed to a short style in the hope that her fans would copy her.

▲Veronica Lake, before and after.

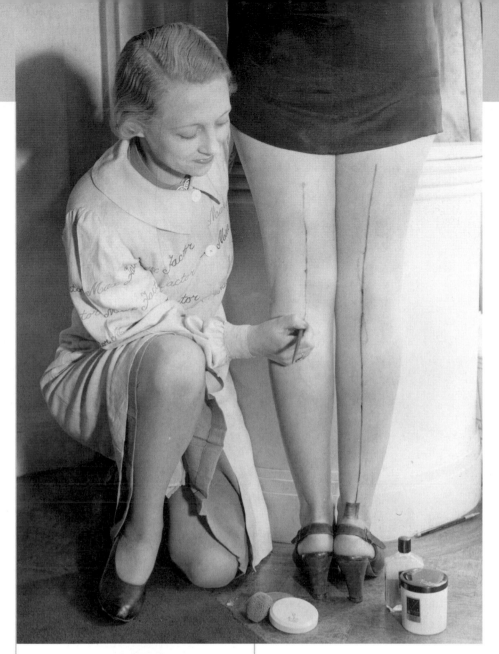

Seams an Illusion

Silk and nylon stockings were in short supply: in Britain, they had vanished from shops completely by December 1940. Pants hid their absence, but women also resorted to Cyclax Stocking-less Cream, or other forms of leg makeup, completing the illusion of stockings by drawing "seams" down the back of the legs with an eyebrow pencil.

When the US War Production Board conducted a survey among American women, asking which cosmetics were absolutely vital to their morale, women agreed that face powder, lipstick, rouge, and deodorant were crucial. Curiously, they also decided that while bath oil was essential, bath salts were not.

▲When it came to appearances, restrictions and shortages brought out the inventive streak in most women.

◄ In this outdoor outfit from Nina Ricci, 1943, the elaborate headgear so common during the war is teamed with a waistline that prefigures the New Look.

►American GIs, new to Britain and encountering shortages for the first time, found themselves much in demand as suppliers of chocolate, cigarettes, and chewing gum.

Paris Under Fire

Occupation

In June 1940, the Germans marched into Paris and occupied the city until August 1944. The French government was taken over by Marshal Philippe Pétain, a veteran of World War I, who asked the Germans for an armistice. It was agreed that a French government, under Pétain, could rule over the unoccupied part of the country. This was known as the Vichy government. Many French people did not recognize its authority, however, because it cooperated with the Germans. Paris and the northern and western parts of France were placed under German rule. Here, as everywhere under Nazi rule, Jewish people were rounded up and deported to concentration and forced labor camps.

The Paris fashion houses were to survive the Nazi occupation of Paris thanks to one man: Lucien Lelong, head of the Chambre Syndicale de la Couture Parisienne (the Paris Fashion Syndicate). Many chief designers and Jewish manufacturers had already left Paris at the outbreak of hostilities, and in 1940 the Berlin High Command ordered the closure of the CSCP and the transfer of the fashion houses and designers to Berlin and Vienna. The Third Reich wanted fashion centers it believed worthy of its leader. Lelong argued that the French

▼A street scene in occupied Paris. Most people seem simply depressed by what is happening to them, although rumors of collaboration with the occupying forces were rife. After the war, society took revenge: a woman suspected of a liaison with a German could expect to have her hair shorn off and her head covered with tar.

▲In occupied France, as in Britain and America, there was a campaign to get women to knit gloves, scarves, and sweaters for soldiers at the front. Most magazines carried approved patterns for various garments.

fashion industry relied not just on the star designers, but also on a whole network of manufacturers and suppliers, expertise that could not be transferred. The order was withdrawn, the Chambre reopened, and Pierre Balmain and Christian Dior moved to join Lelong. In all, twenty fashion houses kept their doors open, and 112,000 skilled workers were excused from compulsory work in enemy factories.

Wedges and Berets

Lelong also pointed out that American clients would bring in much needed dollars—although, in fact, most stayed away for the duration of the war. When rationing was introduced in France in 1941, the fashion houses were given special fabric allowances and permission to sell their garments outside coupon restrictions. Prices soared, not only because of the increased cost of fabric, but also because all other costs now had to be met from a mere hundred styles instead of the prewar level of about 3,000.

The average Parisian woman wore whatever she could get her hands on, and in winter, because of the shortage of fuel, it was all worn at once. Colorful patches and separate collars were a way of enlivening and repairing old clothes, while pants at last became acceptable wear for women. Hefty cork wedges and jointed wooden soles filled the gap left by a scarcity of shoe leather, and by 1943, it seemed that as the wedge heels got higher, hats became more exaggerated to balance the look. Hats with small crowns, upturned brims worn forward and to one side, based on prewar designs by Elsa Schiaparelli, were the order of the day. But perhaps this was a deliberate snub to the unpopular Vichy regime, which in the early 1940s had tried to get its supporters to wear berets.

Haute Couture Collaborators?

When the work done by French fashion designers under German occupation finally came to light, it was greeted with disapproval. It seemed that while everyone else—even Hollywood—had been frugally saving and heeding official regulations, French designers had carried on as if there were no war. The designers' work featured cuffed sleeves, pocket flaps, non-functional buttons, pleats, and draped fabric galore, along with dolman ("parachute" or "magyar") sleeves. The foreign press and buyers were shocked and angry.

And they weren't the only ones. The American War Production Board immediately proposed press censorship, forbidding any reference to Parisian fashions, "which are in flagrant violation of our imposed wartime silhouette," and reminded American manufacturers that L-85 restrictions still applied. No wonder the French government's appeal to the Allied Powers for aid to clothe its population met with a cool response. The Paris designers bowed to the criticisms and the following year limited the fabric in their model dresses to three yards.

Paris Fights Back

The next task was to reassert the importance of Paris as the center of haute couture (high fashion), which began in earnest with the 1945 CSCP's successful

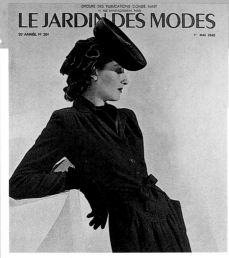

LE JARDIN DES MODES

▲This deceptively simple button-down, shirt waisted day dress by Balenciaga from 1940 benefits from strongly differentiated accessories, especially the eccentric hat.

traveling exhibition, "Le Théâtre de la Mode" (Theater of Fashion), which was shown in the West European capitals and New York. This comprised some 200 dolls, about two feet high, dressed by the leading designers. The observant fashion watcher that year would have seen the way forward. Cristobal Balenciaga brought his hems down to fifteen inches from the floor, and by the following year, most fashion houses had incorporated the narrow waist, more sloping shoulder line, and accentuating of female curves prefigured in 1939 by Mainbocher. But none of this aroused any great excitement or controversy.

That was to come in February 1947 with the Christian Dior show. He brought all the elements together and gave them a new emphasis. The audience went crazy. Carmel Snow, chief editor of *Harper's Bazaar*, summed it up: "It's quite a revolution, dear Christian, your dresses have such a new look." It was these two words—"new look"—that became the international press's name for the dramatic new silhouette.

▲Another day dress, this time from Jacques Heim, shows the military influence in its front detail.

▲If people could not travel to Paris to see the new fashions, then the fashions would have to go to them. The remarkable "Theater of Fashion," with minutely detailed mannequin dolls displayed in a stage setting, toured Europe and the United States.

The American Challenge

American Elegance

With the occupation of Paris by the Germans in June 1940, many people predicted that the center of the fashion world would be transferred to New York. Not only had the atmosphere in prewar Europe already caused a few leading designers from Paris to open salons across the Atlantic, but also a number of American fashion houses were already well established and getting coverage in the fashion magazines. Charles James, Norman Norrell, and Claire McCardell already had their devout followers, and the return of Mainbocher and others from France seemed to seal it. And it wasn't just New York. Dallas, Texas, was getting a name for sportswear and Los Angeles for casual wear, particularly for the beach.

The fact that the Parisian fashion houses were continuing to operate under Nazi occupation suggested to many Americans that money spent on French fashion meant dollars in the Berlin treasury. The New York fashion industry did not simply continue, as before, to follow the lead set by Europe's designers. In 1941, six major department stores in New York City showed American designs twice daily. The race to become top fashion center was on.

For those ladies wanting elegance and glamour, American designer Norman Norell's sequined cocktail dresses were the answer, as was the sophistication of Charles James or the drapery of Mainbocher, former fashion editor and editor of French *Vogue*, who had been designing for Wallis Simpson, Duchess of Windsor, for many years. These designers also had a practical side. Mainbocher worked on uniforms for women attached to the American navy and

▲An extremely glamorous satin evening gown with fur trim, by Mainbocher.

►With money and customers in short supply in war-torn Europe, New York became a haven for the designers of couture evening gowns. These classic and timeless designs are by Anglo-American Charles James.

▼Three models wearing the same gray suit by American designer Claire McCardell from 1943 demonstrate the thrifty way a single outfit could be varied by the addition of different accessories.

Red Cross and promoted knitwear, while Norell explored the growing ready-to-wear market, concentrating on tailored but waistless jersey shifts (which reduced the use of fabric by 50 percent) and the separates look of skirt and shirt, which in 1945 developed into the tightly belted waist and full skirt.

Magnificent McCardell

But the real leader in the free-and-easy style that was the American look was Claire McCardell, who, like Norell, loved the qualities of jersey. She was also a pioneer in the use of unexpected ordinary fabrics, including cotton denim, gingham, calico, and striped mattress ticking. She designed for everywoman and for the everyday world of work and leisure. Her garments were functional and comfortable to wear, with dolman (magyar) sleeves, adjustable waistlines, and deep pockets, in durable or easy-care fabrics. Her Popover dress, designed in 1943, was basically a wraparound denim overall, but it looked so stylish that it remained a favorite well into the fifties. It was classed as a Utility garment, and within a year, 75,000 had been snapped up.

McCardell also hated the clumpy, notoriously difficult to wear wedge and platform shoes, preferring to exploit the US rationing exemption on play shoes and ballet slippers. In 1944, she asked Capezio, the leading New York maker of ballet shoes, to create an outdoor version of their ballet slippers with stronger soles and heels.

The US government regulations on fabric and clothing were quickly lifted after the war. Silk was available again for underclothes and evening wear, although synthetic rayon was still used. An important first was the introduction of nylon stockings that were totally seamless and very sheer, creating a "nude leg" look.

The Changing Silhouette

By 1946, the silhouette began to show definite changes. Shoulders may still have been padded, but some were sloping or dropped, and soon natural, unpadded shoulders became very popular. Opinions were now divided on whether women would opt for a new, radically different style of full and longer skirts or, with their newfound freedom working outside the home, continue to find wartime functional garments more suited to their lifestyle. In a 1947 article, *McCall's* stated: "The short skirt is out of the running. Even before governmental restrictions were taken off skirts, smart girls were letting hems down. The best-looking clothes seen walking around New York at the moment are about fifteen inches from the sidewalks. Fourteen inches if the wearer is short. No two ways about it, hips are very much in style. The new clothes emphasize round

▲The Popover dress revealed Claire McCardell's inventive way with stitched denim.

▼A gold lamé evening dress of stunning simplicity by Norman Norell.

▲ A small waist makes the most of a rounded hipline.

▼Wallis Simpson, Duchess of Windsor, was dressed by Mainbocher for many years and remained a style leader well into middle age.

hips by big pockets, gathers, and drapery. Waistlines are small, and shoulders are rounded."

But it was Dior, supported by the influential fashion journalists Carmel Snow of *Harper's Bazaar* and Mrs. Edna Woolman Chase of *Vogue*, who settled the argument. With his New Look, Paris regained its position as leader of the fashion world for another decade.

▲This two-piece playsuit by American designer Addie Masters is made from synthetic fabric in a rather jazzy pattern.

British Designers at War

Women in Uniform

The recruitment of women into the British armed services from 1938 required new uniforms to be designed, usually based on those of the men. The uniform of the Women's Auxiliary Territorial Service, established in 1938, was similar to that of the British Army, while the Women's Royal Naval Services' uniform was modeled on Royal Navy lines but without the full insignia and markings because, it was argued, the women did not carry out full battle duties. It was recognized that the uniform could affect recruitment and morale. The commander in chief of what was later the Women's Royal Air Force successfully argued for a blue rather than a khaki outfit, partly because of the difficulty in finding cosmetics to match khaki. It was also thought that "blue uniforms would not only encourage loyalty and enthusiasm but would also be an aid to good discipline."

▲British women serving in the navy were the proud wearers of a brand-new uniform, which seems to have allowed for a certain amount of feminine freedom in the hairstyle.

Nurses' uniforms changed dramatically. The Victorian look, with its starched linen—impossible for the battlefront—was increasingly replaced by a simple uniform designed by British designer Norman Hartnell, while the British Red Cross nurse adopted an easy-to-wash gingham outfit.

Digby Morton, an Irish-born fashion designer living in London, worked on the outfit for the Women's Voluntary Service. Established in 1938, the wartime WVS ran soup kitchens at bomb sites, sold tea at ports and stations for the troops, and organized thrift shops for those who had lost everything in the bombing. Green had originally been chosen for the uniform, but since this was traditionally regarded as an unlucky color, gray was added to the weave.

A Boost for Morale

Morale was important on the home front. The British government recognized that stringent rationing could quickly demoralize the population, and in 1942, with only a little prodding, the country's fashion designers, along with Captain Edward Molyneux from France, were brought together in the Incorporated Society of

▲Senior British designer Norman Hartnell was a founder member of the group that masterminded the Utility program.

◄ Mr. and Mrs. Average—Utility designs for men and women from 1945.

▲Stripes and checks serve to brighten up an otherwise simply cut outfit, but note the wrap-and-tie detail, which cinches in the waist and emphasizes the flare of the unpressed pleats.

London Fashion Designers. Members included Hardy Amies, Norman Hartnell, Digby Morton, and Victor Stiebel, and their task was to show that, despite rationing, clothes could still be fashionable and attractive. They came up with the Utility collection—stylish garments that conformed to the government regulations. From their designs for four basic items—a coat, a suit, an afternoon dress, and a cotton dress suitable for office work—thirty-two were selected for production in 1943. The line was essentially based on prewar styling and retained the heavy square-shouldered look of the late 1930s, although—while staying within fabric restrictions—jackets and tops had a slightly bloused look. When worn with pants or skirts lacking fullness and hats modeled on cap and beret shapes, the designs had a distinctly military look.

▲Although most of the wool produced went into the manufacture of uniforms, home knitting was greatly encouraged, and sweaters became popular.

Can Make It—Can't Have It!

Although deprived of their usual business of dressing the British aristocracy, the members of the ISLFD continued their haute couture work, but now solely for overseas customers. Because the promotion of British designs and fabrics like Harris tweed brought in badly needed dollars, this had full government approval. Peacetime brought no immediate change, and the mass of visitors seeing the new ISLFD fashion styles at London's Victoria & Albert Museum in the spring of 1946 discovered from the catalog that virtually everything on display was for export only. The exhibition's official title, "Britain Can Make It," was soon popularly changed to "Britain Can't Have It."

▲Definitely a non-Utility design! The British cartoon "Just Jane" provided comic fantasy relief for troops and others with her scandalous adventures. Here she prepares for the rigors of war in 1940 by swapping her thirties-style evening gown for a uniform.

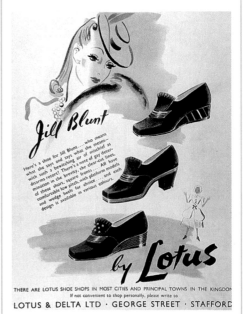

▲Wedge heels for wartime wear from the Lotus company in 1941.

▲ A model shows off a new tweed trouser suit by DAKS, classic British designers of casual and leisure wear since 1894.

▲Women workers at a spark plug factory in Britain, 1941, wearing special hats and snoods to prevent hair from becoming tangled in machinery.

▲ Utility fashions for the British company Berkatex by Norman Hartnell, 1943.

While American and French high fashion recognized the high quality of British export textiles, the runways of the ISLFD salons offered no serious competition at this time to those of Paris and New York, and not just because rationing was still in force. From their memoirs and biographies, it seems most of the British designers did not consider this period of austerity their "finest hour" and preferred, on the whole, to forget it.

Zoot-suiters, Spivs, and Zazous

Zoot-suiters

There is still some dispute about exactly where the zoot suit fashion began. The name may have been coined by American bandleader and clothier Harold Fox in 1942, but whatever its origin, the style was favored by both black and Hispanic teenagers in New York's Harlem and on the West Coast. It consisted of a knee-length draped jacket with six-inch shoulder pads, an eye-catching tie (bow or knotted), a long dangling key chain, and very high-waisted trousers, fully and deeply pleated at the waist and generous in the leg but sharply tapered at the cuff. The look was completed with a long, greased hairstyle, combed back off the face, a broad brimmed hat, and pointed-toe shoes.

◄ Jazz musicians, often considered to be on the edge of polite society, began to cultivate an "alternative" image. Here trumpeter Dizzy Gillespie sports a double-breasted suit, goatee beard, and black beret.

►Cab Calloway, resident orchestra leader at New York's famous Cotton Club, in classic zoot-suit: long, draped jacket, baggy pants with narrow cuffs, and dangling key chain.

▲Note especially the two-tone shoes worn by the snappily dressed entourage in this typical nightclub routine.

Perhaps it was the zoot-suiters' apparent disregard of austerity regulations to which the servicemen of Chavez Ravine military base in California took exception when, for two nights in June 1943, they savagely beat up the Mexican zoot-suiters of Los Angeles. They cut their hair and stripped off their trousers while the naval shore patrol and army military police looked the other way.

►The chalk-stripe suit beloved of gangsters and postwar wide boys. The wide-brimmed hat, two-tone shoes, and patterned tie provide the essential accessories.

In his letter to the president, demanding the arrest and punishment of the servicemen involved, political commentator Walter White brought out some of the social significance of the fashion when he stated that the zoot-suiters dressed as they did "to compensate for the sense of being neglected by society. The wearers are almost invariably the victims of poverty, proscription, and segregation."

▲The *zazou* style may have been a fleeting fashion, but on the streets of Paris, it could hardly be ignored.

Zazous

A similar fashion was seen on the streets of occupied Paris among the zazous, streetwise people involved in the black market and general racketeering. Only through those illegal connections could the men acquire their huge dropped-shouldered, thigh-length jackets and tight, almost drainpipe trousers and the women the square-shouldered fur coats, short skirts, and striped stockings in which they paraded the streets. Both carried large umbrellas and peered through dark sunglasses whatever the weather. But by 1945, a year after the liberation of Paris, the zazou style was finished and the secondhand shops in Paris were full of this now unfashionable clothing.

Spivs

Confusion surrounds the phenomenon of the British "spiv", or "wide boy", although it is clear why he emerged. He was the small-time black-market racketeer who, for a price, could get anything you couldn't find in the shops. So, as rationing became more rigorous, he appeared more frequently in the town centers with his battered suitcase or handcart full of things that had "fallen off the back of a truck." Where the terms spiv and wide boy came from, and whether his style of dress can be linked with the American zoot suit is unclear. *Picture Post* stated that the word spiv came from Detroit in the 1920s, while others maintain it is from the Welsh *spilav*, meaning "to push." As for wide boy, that may refer to the wide chalk-striped suiting material that was worn by many spivs. This fabric had been first popularized by Edward VIII when he was Duke of Windsor but had fallen out of favor with his abdication in 1936.

The style is usually described as "flashy," but contemporary cartoons show the spiv's suit was usually well tailored from good-quality material, whereas the average man's suit in postwar Britain looked shabby and ill fitting. The generous wide lapels and double-breasted look of the spiv jacket spoke of money, and the jacket was worn with a wide, colorful tie, a little trilby hat (made of felt, with a lengthwise dent in the crown and a narrow brim) worn to one side over the forehead. The spiv no longer sported the flamboyant handlebar mustache beloved of the wartime Royal Air Force but instead the tiny, neatly trimmed mustache popularized by Hollywood's Ronald Colman.

Men at War and Peace

GI Joe

It wasn't really until American GIs—the abbreviation stands for "government issue" but was used generally to denote American servicemen—were seen over in Britain that people realized how ill fitting the British military uniforms were. The GIs all looked like officers in their stylish uniforms, while the British field dress, with its high-waisted long jacket and baggy trousers, appeared crumpled alongside its American counterpart. It didn't help, either, that to save cloth and production costs, details like pocket pleats and pointed sleeve cuffs had been dropped, and the smarter ceremonial dress was no longer in production.

Everyday menswear was also regulated under both the British Utility scheme and the American L-85 order. The only exception was the clothing provided for undercover intelligence officers sent into enemy territory—such

►The duffle coat, one of the most essential additions to the civilian wardrobe from the war years, would continue to go in and out of fashion for decades to come.

▼British servicemen are shown their demob outfits. There was very little choice, and in style, not much had changed since the thirties. Many joked that they had simply exchanged one uniform for another.

austere styling worn abroad would have immediately identified the wearers as spies and agents. Some garments that disappeared during the war never came back into fashion, while others born of necessity became standards. Vests, for instance, used up valuable coupons in Britain and were banned under American restrictions, but short socks introduced to save wool remained in fashion after 1945. The shortage of wool also led to the introduction of very tight-fitting sweaters with a short body length.

Back to Peacetime

With the coming of peace, more than 5 million British servicemen were demobilized, that is, released from military service. The desperate clothing shortage in Britain meant that the social niceties of wearing a special outfit appropriate to different occasions was largely forgotten. Ordinary everyday suits, called lounge suits, were now perfectly acceptable for all occasions, and everyone accepted that the scarcity of dyestuffs meant that suit material came in lighter tones. In the United States, *The New Yorker* magazine wittily illustrated seven outfits, complete with hats, that the returning soldier would need for leisure and work—but that, of course, he couldn't possibly afford.

As rationing ended, men celebrated by selecting double-breasted suit jackets and coats with wide, peaked lapels, so popular before the war. Trousers again became fuller in the leg. Cuffs reappeared, as did unpressed pleats at the waist. At first, the trouser waist was high, as in prewar styles, but gradually, it was lowered. Men on both sides of the Atlantic also took to wearing items of military dress, notably the duffle coat in Britain and in the United States, the T-shirt.

Duffle Coats

Although Viscount Montgomery of Alamein—the British commander in chief in the North African, Normandy, and Ardennes campaigns—was frequently seen wearing a duffle coat, what made this garment truly popular was its association with the merchant navy and the small, fast escort ships called corvettes, which plied the Atlantic, immortalized in Nicholas Monserrat's novel and the subsequent film *The Cruel Sea,* in 1952. Subzero temperatures and wave-washed decks dictated the duffle's wooden toggles and hemp (rope) loops, which frozen fingers could manage more easily than metal fastenings and buttonholes.

▲General Eisenhower, observing troops prior to the invasion of Europe, sports a version of the American "reefer" coat.

After the war, these thick woolen navy coats, named after their original place of manufacture, Duffel in Flanders, were snapped up from military surplus stores. It was only when they were adopted by university teachers and students and increasingly associated with the anti-establishment in the late fifties that the duffle coat lost its heroic aura and became the badge of the intellectual.

ADAM, La Revue de l'Homme   HIVER 1943-44   Reproduction interdite

▲Stylish overcoats, in a rather English-looking tweed, for the French man about town of 1943. The dog is probably an optional extra.

▲Sports clothes from California, 1947: a checked wool jacket with patch pockets and four-button front, worn with cuffed slacks and a tailored sports shirt.

T-shirts

The Japanese attack on Pearl Harbor had the immediate result of putting eleven million Americans into uniform—and into regulation underwear. The following year, the US Navy sent out its official specifications for an undershirt—calling it a T-type shirt—with a round neck and short sleeves set in at right angles to the front and back panels, made in knitted cotton. At first, they were plain white but were later often printed with the name of the military base or division.

The prewar fashion for sleeveless undershirts had gone into decline after Clark Gable appeared without one in the film *It Happened One Night* (1934). Suddenly, it was unmanly to wear that kind of undershirt. The T-shirt, however, saw so much battle action that no one could think the same about this garment. By the time a T-shirted Marlon Brando was acclaimed for his "sensual, unfeeling, mean, vindictive performance" in *A Streetcar Named Desire* (1951), the T-shirt's success was sealed.

▶The T-shirt, another military garment that quickly gained a place in the wardrobes of returning GIs, was given a huge boost at the turn of the decade when worn by Marlon Brando.

Hollywood

Impact

The Hollywood studio costume designer had to wrestle with a set of problems different from those facing the haute couture houses. Designs had to pass a censorship board called the Hays Office, set up to guard against provocative costumes, as well as enforce conformity to the government's austerity program, and determine whether to conceal or emphasize the physical attributes of the individual star.

Devices intended to flatter a star's looks had sometimes spawned long-lived popular fashions, such as designer Adrian's decision to accentuate Joan Crawford's broad shoulders—in *Letty Lynton* (1932) and *Today We Live* (1933)—to make her hips seem narrower. His trademark square shoulders and short skirts were so influential that those responsible for drawing up the L-85 order and Utility program could not envisage women's fashions without padding. And not only the costume designer had an impact. Filmmaker Howard Hughes is credited with having designed the wired brassiere worn by Jane Russell in *The Outlaw* (1943) in order to get the contour and exaggerated uplift he required.

▶Designer Adrian was a favorite of Hollywood stars. This outfit typifies the elaborate and three-dimensional tailoring for which he became known. Based on the broad-shouldered silhouette, the suit displays an intriguing asymmetrical cut.

▶Scarlett O'Hara's green velvet dress, cut from a pair of curtains, was Hollywood's ultimate symbol of "make do and mend" home fashion.

Sex symbol Jane Russell set the screen smoldering in *The Outlaw*. To make the most of her curvaceous figure, most of her screen outfits were made of tight-fitting jersey or other softly clinging fabrics.

Hollywood goes to War

War brought its own problems, with hundreds of studio staff diverted into war work and those who remained having to work with slashed budgets and other restrictions. The supply of shiny bugle beads, so essential to the glitzy Hollywood look, was totally cut off by Hitler's invasion of Czechoslovakia, where the beads originated. By 1942, studio stocks of brocades, gold and silver lamé, satin, and crepe were severely depleted, and as rationing came into force, wardrobe departments were ransacked for old costumes that could be taken apart and restyled for new productions. The famous scene in *Gone with the Wind* —made in 1939 and still showing to packed movie houses in the 1940s—in which Scarlett O'Hara (Vivien Leigh) makes a dress from green velvet curtains took on a whole new significance.

All points to Glamour

Hollywood's most obvious impact was, as ever, on the glamour business. A picture of Betty Grable in a one-piece swimsuit, looking over her shoulder at the camera, was one of the most popular pinups among the American forces, although the alluring Rita Hayworth came a close second. But while many women may have envied the legs of Betty Grable, few wanted to imitate the "Brazilian

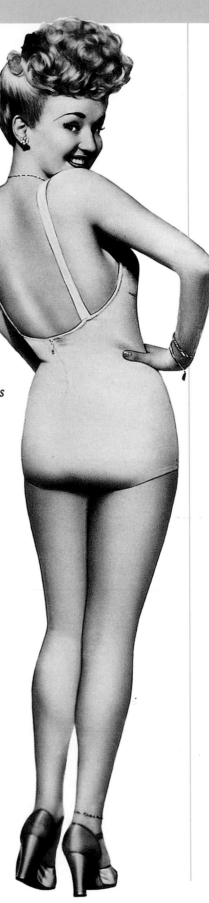

◄The big-shouldered look spreads to romantic evening wear: girl-next-door Deanna Durbin all dressed up in *Nice Girl?* (1941).

►Betty Grable's famous legs made her the armed forces' favorite pin-up.

▼The elegant costumes worn by Judy Garland and her screen family in *Meet Me in St. Louis* (1944) may look like silk, but the ever resourceful studio wardrobe actually used rayon as a look-alike substitute.

▲Dorothy Lamour on the road to somewhere exotic in one of the sarongs that she single-handedly made famous.

bombshell," Carmen Miranda, who was most famously seen with exotic displays of fruit balanced on her head. Nevertheless, Miranda certainly played her part in promoting the turban, so necessary for factory safety, as a glamour item. Her wedge shoes, too, were closely copied by shoe manufacturers, while the taste for Latin American frills and off-the-shoulder peasant blouses and "Pacific" sarong prints was stimulated by the *Road* films starring Dorothy Lamour, Bob Hope, and Bing Crosby.

Less exotic fashions were typified by the white organdy dress designed by Vera West for Deanna Durbin in *Nice Girl?* (1941), which was copied endlessly for American prom dances, and the rose-covered hats worn in the war film *Mrs. Miniver* (1942)—a fashion that spread eventually to Paris. As for menswear, films such as *This Gun for Hire,* with Alan Ladd, and *Casablanca*, with Humphrey Bogart, ensured the popularity of the trench coat with the belt casually tied and the collar up.

But movie fashion didn't like restraint, and within months of Germany and Japan surrendering, Hollywood returned to extravagance.

▶Top-to-toe fashion from the exotic Carmen Miranda.

The New Look

The Feminine Image

For Christian Dior, his February 1947 collection symbolized a new beginning based on nostalgia for the Belle Epoque, a period of comfortable life just before World War I: "We were emerging from a period of war, of uniforms, of women-soldiers built like boxers. I drew women-flowers, soft shoulders, flowering busts, fine waists like liana [slender vines] and wide skirts like corolla [flowers]." It was a look that symbolized opulence, wealth, and femininity, in clear contrast to the wartime outline. The shape looked natural, but was in reality totally artificial, entailing as it did shoulder and hip pads, a padded bra, and a boned waist girdle.

▲The new look didn't come without a price, however. The shoulder pads, wasp-waist corset, and hip pads required to underpin the new feminine silhouette were, not surprisingly, often referred to as "armor plating."

◄ Dior's classic New Look day wear: a tapering jacket with tightly fitted waist, paired with pleated full skirt, hat, and gloves. Demure and ladylike, this was about as far as one could get from the fashions of the war years.

◄ And the New Look certainly wasn't universally popular. Here the style gets some dirty looks in New York as a demonstration is mounted against the extravagant new style for the benefit of Marguerite Cook, model and devotee of the new hemlines, in October 1947.

Counting the Cost

It wasn't just the corsetry that caused the temperature of public and government alike to soar abroad: it was the cost of the vast amount of fabric used in making the skirt; often over twenty-five yards. Even in Paris, women demonstrated, angrily shouting, "Forty thousand francs for a dress and our children have no milk!" At the time, a schoolteacher earned 9,000 francs a month and dairy products, oils, and chocolate were still rationed.

Given the limited amount of material available overall, estimates showed that the cloth needed for Dior's new length and fullness would bring output down by the equivalent of 800,000 garments manufactured in regulation style. The president of the British Board of Trade warned that since it would be impossible to make and sell the same number of garments, the whole future of the British economy was at stake, and he persuaded the British Guild of Creative Designers to boycott the new length. A female member of Parliament, Mabel Ridealgh, denounced the style as "too reminiscent of the 'caged bird' attitude," adding, "I hope our fashion dictators will realize the new outlook of women and give the death blow to any attempt at curtailing women's freedom." A female press commentator railed: "We are back in the days when fashion was the prerogative of the leisured wealthy woman, and not the everyday concern of typist, saleswoman, or housewife"—pointing out that few British women had the fabric allowance, the money, or the personal lifestyle that suited the New Look.

Dior Triumphant

But most British women in the late forties had had enough of their Utility wardrobes and wanted change. On hearing the news that rationing was to be continued, Marghanita Laski summed up their feelings in British *Vogue*: "Patriotism is definitely NOT ENOUGH, and I, for one, am fed up. I'm fed up at home and I'm fed up when I go abroad, I don't like to see a foreigner pointing

▲A tiny waist, tapering shoulders, full three-quarter-length skirt, and high-heeled court shoes: the overall silhouette could be adapted for day, evening, or outerwear.

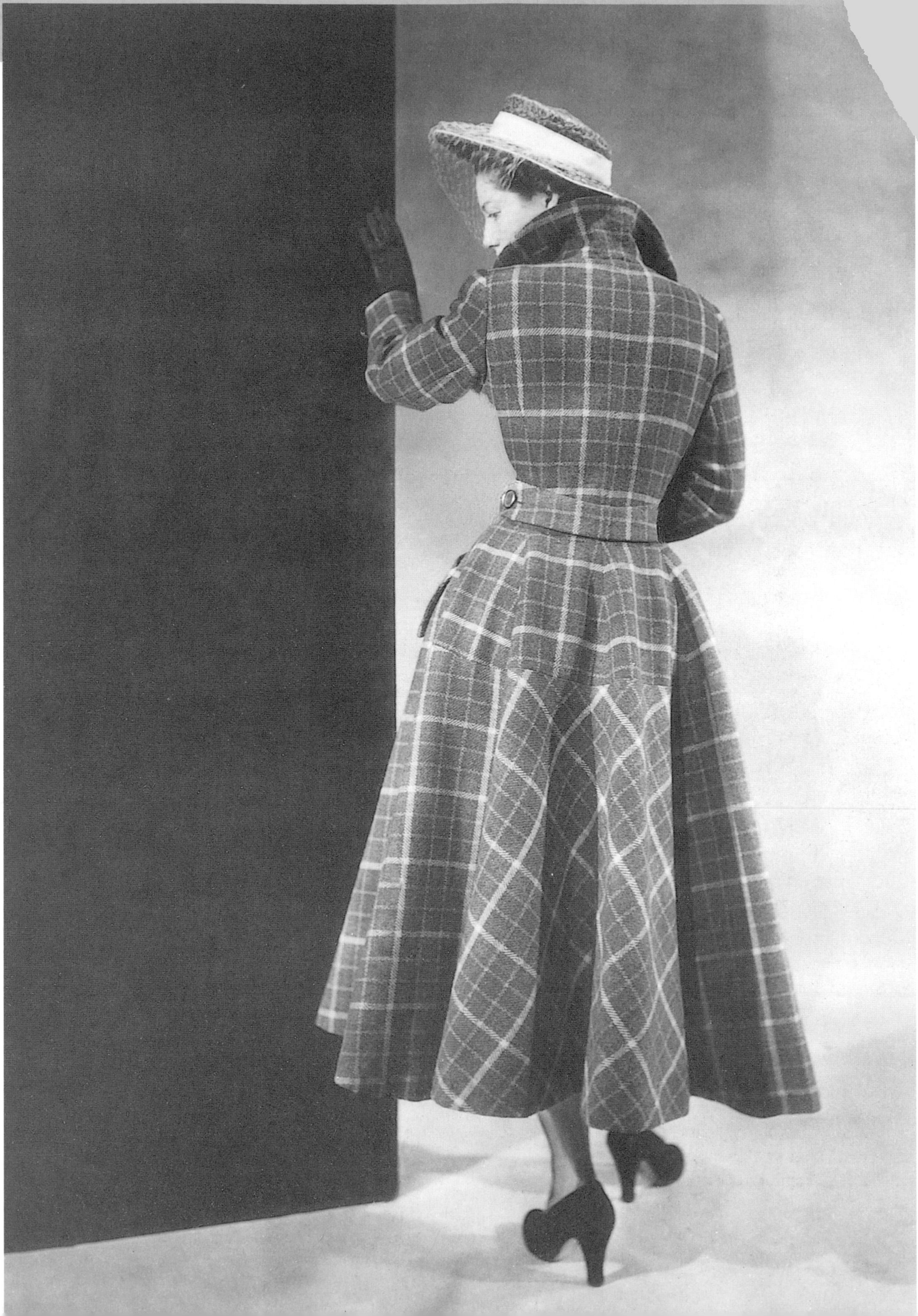

and whispering, "You can see she's English—look at her clothes!" And if Princess Margaret, then seventeen, could appear in public with an extra band of fabric sewn onto her coat hem to achieve the new length, so could others. By 1948, London department stores were selling garments based on Dior's designs for six British pounds with fifteen coupons. In no time, everything had a New Look label, including furniture, housing, and even a kind of daffodil.

American women were also hostile at first to the new length, although it has been suggested that this was because it hid their legs. American designer Adrian locked horns on American radio with Mrs. Chase from *Vogue* over the New Look. Mrs. Chase and Carmel Snow of *Harper's Bazaar* were passionate advocates of Dior, while Adrian bitterly criticized the American fashion magazines for suddenly transferring their loyalty back to Paris and welcoming the reintroduction of heavy corsetry.

But he lost the argument, and the United States lost its battle to be the center of the fashion world. Paris, led by Dior, had won. Rumor had it that the longer length had simply been a means of increasing sales for Dior's financial backer, textile industrialist Marcel Boussac. Whatever the truth was, six years after its establishment, the fashion house of Dior had expanded into six companies, sixteen associated enterprises, twenty-eight workrooms, and over 1,000 employees. The New Look was to influence the world of haute couture for ten years.

▲Hattie Carnegie gives another American version of the style in 1948. Following the established silhouette, it is the choice of colors and detail decoration that gives this design its individual stamp.

▲Paul Parnes provides an American interpretation of the New Look in fall 1947. For autumn warmth, full-length dresses were combined with suit jackets in Parnes's collections.

◄ This gun-metal-and-pale-blue-check tweed coat by British designer Hardy Amies is a world away from his Utility collection. High-heeled court shoes were essential to balance the classic silhouette of the New Look.

Chronology

1940

News

Nazi forces invade Denmark, Holland, and Belgium.
Paris is occupied.
British prime minister Neville Chamberlain resigns, and Winston Churchill takes over.

1941

The Soviet Union fights off the Nazi invasion.
The Japanese attack on Pearl Harbor destroys nineteen ships and 120 aircraft.

1942

The United States enters the war.
Battle of El Alamein checks the German and Italian advance in North Africa.

1943

Death camps established in Nazi Europe.
Italy surrenders: downfall of Mussolini.

1944

Allied forces liberate France.

1945

U.S. President Franklin Delano Roosevelt dies.
Hitler commits suicide, and premier Benito Mussolini is shot. Nazi Germany surrenders, as does Japan, following the bombing of Hiroshima and Nagasaki.

1946

Nuclear tests take place on Bikini Atoll.
In Britain, the National Health Service is introduced.

1947

India achieves independence.
Princess Elizabeth marries Philip Mountbatten in a Norman Hartnell dress.

1948

Olympic Games are held in London after a twelve-year break.
The State of Israel is established.

1949

The People's Republic of China is formally proclaimed.
The North Atlantic Treaty Organization (NATO) is established.

Events

Food rationing begins in Britain and in occupied France.

Aerosols are patented.
First commercial TV networks in the United States begin broadcasting.

Large-scale production of penicillin helps the recovery of war casualties.

The Outlaw, starring Jane Russell, is filmed, but its release is delayed for three years.

Betty Grable is voted top woman film star; Bing Crosby is top male film star.
Charlie Parker, Thelonius Monk, and others begin classic sound of bebop jazz recordings.

American wartime rationing is removed.
George Orwell's *Animal Farm* is a best seller.

The phrase "Iron Curtain" is used by Churchill in a speech in the United States.
The word *teenager* is coined in the monthly magazine *Mayfair*.

A Boeing 377 Stratocruiser becomes the first postwar transatlantic plane to carry fifty passengers across the Atlantic.

First solar-heated house is built.
Transistors are invented.
First microwave ovens are in use.

First TV westerns appear.

Fashion

Schiaparelli takes her collection to the United States, the last French collection to be shown abroad for five years.
Norell and McCardell steal the (fashion) show in New York.

The British government bans the sale of silk stockings.
Clothes rationing is introduced in Great Britain.

The U.S. government imposes clothing restrictions under the L-85 order.
In London, the ISLFD produces the first Utility fashions, which go into production in 1943.

The British media campaign "Make Do and Mend" starts.
Claire McCardell's denim Popover dress proves very popular.

Foreign journalists react badly to Paris fashion shows. British and American governments ban wide-scale media coverage of the Paris designs.

Schiaparelli returns to Paris. Balmain reopens his salon.
Balenciaga drops the hemline to fifteen inches off the ground, anticipating Dior's New Look.

The bikini swimsuit is shown in Paris.
"Britain Can Make It" exhibition is shown in London.
Molyneux reopens his salon in Paris.

The House of Dior opens with the New Look, which is very well received.

Growth of mass-production garment manufacturing occurs, with styles based on Dior's designs.

A new dance beat—Rhythm and Blues—is emerging.
In Britain, clothes rationing largely disappears.

Glossary

Adrian (Gilbert Adrian) (1903–59) At first known for his theater and film costumes, dressing such stars as Joan Crawford, Greta Garbo, and Katharine Hepburn, Adrian moved into the haute couture world by opening a salon in 1941 in Beverly Hills. His work favored heavily padded shoulders, a clear waistline, and clever diagonal closings.

Amies, Hardy (1909–2003) British born, Amies was known for his tailored suits and lavish ball gowns, designed for ladies of the British aristocracy and royal family. While serving in British Army Intelligence during the war, he contributed designs to the ISLFD.

Balenciaga, Cristobal (1895–1972) By the early 1930s, Balenciaga was Spain's leading fashion designer but he moved to Paris in 1936, returning to his homeland during World War II. With his dramatic designs in strong, rich colors, he is held by many fashion commentators to be the great innovator of the postwar period.

Balmain, Pierre (1914–82) French born, Balmain worked with Molyneux and Lelong before opening his own salon in 1945. With a reputation for elegant tailoring, he quickly realized the sales potential of boutique accessories and the ready-to-wear market.

Carnegie, Hattie (1889–1956) While employed as a shop assistant at Macy's in New York, Carnegie designed hats. She opened her millinery shop in 1909, followed six years later by a dressmaking salon. Although she herself closely followed Paris fashions, she was responsible for discovering and nurturing the talent of James Galanos, Norman Norell, and Claire McCardell.

Dior, Christian (1905–57) This French designer first worked with Piguet and Lelong. He had instant success with his first one-man collection, the Corolla Line (renamed the New Look), in 1947. He continued to exert great influence on the haute couture world until his death in 1957, by which time his salon had expanded into a multi-million-dollar fashion business.

Hartnell, (Sir) Norman (1901–79) Hartnell, a British designer, showed his first collection in Paris in 1927. He was appointed dressmaker to the British royal family in 1938, designing both the wedding dress and coronation robes for Princess Elizabeth. He helped found the ISLFD, and a number of his designs were manufactured under the Utility label. Although well known for his embroidered evening gowns and tailored suits, he also designed the officers' dress uniform of the Women's Royal Army Corps and that of the British Red Cross.

Incorporated Society of London Fashion Designers (ISLFD) The ISLFD was founded in 1942 to promote British fashion abroad and assist the coordination between government, manufacturers, and fashion houses, particularly during the war years. Besides Captain Molyneux, its chairman for many years, other members included Amies, Hartnell, and Digby Morton. Very influential in the 1940s, ISLFD's heyday was in the early sixties, when British fashion stole the scene.

James, Charles (1906–78) James first entered the fashion world as a milliner, working under the name of Boucheron, in Chicago. After moving to New York and then London, he settled in Paris until the outbreak of war in 1939, when he returned to New York. He put great emphasis on the cut and seaming of garments, often working in heavy silks. He retired in 1958 to continue his work as an artist and sculptor.

Lelong, Lucien (1889–1958) One of the first French designers to work in the ready-to-wear sector, Lelong became president of the Chambre Syndicale de la Couture in 1937, a post he was to hold for ten years until ill health forced him to retire and close his salon. It was his skillful negotiations with the Berlin High Command that ensured the survival of the Parisian fashion houses. His own salon, which reopened in 1941, was staffed with Dior and Balmain, among others.

Mainbocher (Main Rousseau Bocher) (1891–1976) An American designer, Mainbocher worked in London, Munich, and Paris. First a fashion artist and journalist, he then became editor of *Vogue* (French edition) and designed for Wallis Simpson, Duchess of Windsor, before retiring in 1971. His collection in 1939, shortly before his return to the United States, anticipated Dior's postwar New Look. Famous for his ball gowns and evening sweaters, he also designed uniforms for the American Red Cross, WAVES, SPARS (the U.S. Coast Guard's Women's Reserve), and Girl Scouts.

McCardell, Claire (1905–58) This American designer favored a functional look in practical fabrics. She is considered to have been one of the United States' most influential designers for the modern career woman.

Molyneux, Captain Edward (1891–1974) After gaining experience in a British fashion house and seeing active service in World War I, Molyneux opened his salon in Paris in 1919. His fluid elegant designs were worn by Princess Marina, Gertrude Lawrence, and Merle Oberon, among others. Escaping to England at the outbreak of war, he joined the ISLFD, becoming its president, and was a committed advocate of training and education for fashion students. His Paris salon reopened in 1946, but his ill health forced its closure in 1949.

Norell, Norman (1900–72) American born, Norell became well known for his Hollywood and Broadway costume designs from the twenties, and his sequin-sheath evening dresses remained a firm favorite in American society circles for many years. He was the founder and president of the Council of Fashion Designers of America.

Schiaparelli, Elsa (1890–1973) Born in Italy, Schiaparelli lived in the United States until 1918, when she moved to Paris and started designing knitwear. By 1930, she was employing 2,000 people in twenty-six workrooms. Her approach to fabrics and accessories was unconventional and innovative. A lecture tour of the United States took her away from Paris before its occupation, but she returned in 1945 to reopen her salon, retiring in 1954.

Further Reading

A great deal has been written and published about the 1940s—this reading list is only a very small selection. Magazines and movies of the period are another excellent source of information.

Adult General Reference Sources

Calasibetta, Charlotte. *Essential Terms of Fashion: A Collection of Definitions* (Fairchild, 1985).

Calasibetta, Charlotte. *Fairchild's Dictionary of Fashion* (Fairchild, 2nd ed, 1988).

Cumming, Valerie. *Understanding Fashion History* (Chrysalis, 2004)

Ewing, Elizabeth. *History of Twentieth Century Fashion*, revised by Alice Mackrell (Batsford, 4th ed, 2001)

Gold, Annalee. *90 Years of Fashion* (Fairchild, 1990).

Laver, James. *Costume and Fashion* (Thames & Hudson, 1995)

Martin, Richard. *American Ingenuity: Sportswear 1930s-1970s* (Yale, 1998)

O'Hara, Georgina. *The Encyclopedia of Fashion* (Harry N. Abrams, 1986).

Olian, JoAnne. *Everyday Fashions of the Forties as pictured in Sears Catalogs* (Dover, 1992)

Peacock, John. *Twentieth Century Fashion: The Complete Sourcebook* (Thames & Hudson, 1993)

Peacock, John. *Fashion Sourcebook: The Forties* (Thames & Hudson, 1998)

Peacock, John. *Men's Fashion: The Complete Sourcebook* (Emerald, 1997)

Peacock, John. *Fashion Accessories: The Complete 20th Century Sourcebook* (Thames & Hudson 2000)

Skinner, Tina. *Fashionable Clothing from Sears Catalogs: early 40s-80s* (Schiffer, 2004)

Steele, Valerie. *Fifty Years of Fashion: New Look to Now* (Yale, 2000)

Stegemeyer, Anne. *Who's Who in Fashion,* (Fairchild, 4th ed, 2003)

Trahey, Jane (ed.) *100 Years of the American Female from Harper's Bazaar* (Random House, 1967).

Watson, Linda. *Twentieth-century Fashion* (Firefly, 2004)

Young Adult Sources

Reynolds, Helen. *Twentieth Century Fashion: the 40s and 50s* (Heinemann Library, 1999)

Ruby, Jennifer. *The Nineteen Forties & Nineteen Fifties, Costume in Context series* (David & Charles, 1989)

Wilcox, R. Turner. *Five Centuries of American Costume* (Scribner's, 1963).

Acknowledgments

The Publishers would like to thank the following for permission to reproduce illustrations: B.T. Batsford 14, 19l, 20, 30r 34l, 37, 39br, 41l, 43bl, 44r, 46, 49, 51t, 52, 56l, 56r, 58, 59l; Bettmann Archive 25t, 36b; Corbis 36t, 39bl; David Redfern 25b, 44l; Fashion Institute 38t, 38b, 39t; Getty Images 8, 31t, 50l; Getty/Time Life 29t; Keystone 22t, 22b; Kobal Collection 12t, 30bl, 30br, 51b, 54bl, 55l, 55r; Library of Congress 23, 27; Lighthorne Pictures 42tr, 42br; Mary Evans Picture Library 18b, 28b, 50r; National Film Archive 53b, 54tl, 54r; Pictorial Press 53t; Popperfoto 11, 12b, 29b, 30t, 31bl, 32, 40t, 40b, 41r, 42l, 43tl, 43r, 48, 57t, 57b; Retrograph 7, 16t, 19r, 33, 34r, 59r; Robert Opie Collection 13t, 13b, 31br; Topfoto 9, 10, 16b, 17, 28t, 35, 47; Victoria & Albert Museum 45; Vintage Magazine Co. 6, 15, 18t, 21l, 21r, 24, 26

Key: b=bottom, t=top, l=left, r=right

Index

Figures in *italics* refer to illustrations.

Adrian 52, *52*, 59
American War Production Board 33
Amies, Hardy 41, *58*
Astor, Lady 9

Balenciaga, Cristobal 34, *34*
Balmain, Pierre 33
Battle of Britain 6
bikini 19, *19*
Board of Trade 12, 57
bobby sox *16*, *25*
Bogart, Humphrey 55
Boussac, Marcel 59
Bowles, Chester 10
Brando, Marlon 51
British Guild of Creative Designers 57
British Red Cross 40

Calloway, Cab *44*
capes *19*
Carnegie, Hattie 21, *59*
Chambre Syndicale de la Couture Parisienne 32
Chanel, Gabrielle "Coco" 9, *9*
Chase, Mrs. Edna Woolman 39, 59
Colman, Ronald 47
Cook, Marguerite *57*
Cooper, Gary 17
cosmetics 31, 40
coveralls 14, 30, *30*
Crosby, Bing 25, 55

Dallas 36
dickeys 28
Dior, Christian 19, *19*, 22, *22*, 33, 34, 39, 56, *56*, 57, 59
dolman sleeves 33, 38
duffle coats 48, 49, *49*, 50
Durbin, Deanna *54*, 55

Edward VIII 47
Elizabeth II 9

Fox, Harold 44
fur 12, *36*, 47

Gable, Clark 51
gas-protection suits 8
girdles 29, 30, 56
GIs 14, 31, 48, 51
gloves 6, *10*, *19*, *21*, 27, 28, *33*, *56*
Goodman, Benny *8*
Goodrich, B. F. 24
Grable, Betty 53, 54

hairstyles *15*, *29*, 30
handbags 28
Hartnell, Norman 10, *11*, 40, *40*, 41, *43*
hats 6, *10*, *21*, *27*, 30, 33, *34*, *43*, *46*, 47, 55, *56*
Hays Office 52
head scarves 6, *30*
Hiroshima 19, 21
Hitler, Adolf 6
Hollywood fashions 52–55
Hughes, Howard 52

Incorporated Society of London Fashion Designers 12, 40

jabots 28
James, Charles 17, 36, *36*
Jantzen 23

King, Muriel *20*
Koroseal *24*

Lake, Veronica 30, *30*
Lamour, Dorothy 55
Laski, Marghanita 57
Leigh, Vivien 53, *53*
Lelong, Lucien 10, 32, 33
Los Angeles 36, 45
lounge suits 49

Mainbocher 12, 34, 36, *36*, *39*
Margaret, Princess 59
Masters, Addie *39*
Maxwell, Vera 30
McCardell, Claire 36, *36*, 38, *38*
military demobilization clothes *16*, 17, *48*
Miranda, Carmen 55, *55*
Molyneux, Edward 40
Morton, Digby 40, 41

New York 6, 12, *12*, *22*, 34, 36, *37*, 38, 43, 44, *44*, *57*
Norell, Norman *23*, 36, 38, *38*
nurses 40
nylon 10, 31, 38

pants for women 33, 40
Paris 9, *9*, 10, 12, 13, 19, 32, *32*, 33, 36, 39, 47, *47*
Parnes, Paul 59
Pearl Harbor 6, 51
Pétain, Marshal Philippe 32
Popover dress 38, *38*

rationing
  clothes 9, 19, 28, 33, 38, 40, 41, 43, 47, 53, 57
  food 10, 13, *13*
rayon 38, *54*
Rear, Louis 19
Reed, Austin *21*
Ricci, Nina *31*
Ridealgh, Mabel 57
Rosenstein, Nettie *20*
rubber 29
Russell, Jane 52, *53*

Schiaparelli, Elsa 33
sequins 10, 36
sheepskin jackets 17, *17*
Sheridan, Ann 12, *12*
shoes 6, *30*, 38, *42*, 44, *45*, *46*, 55, *57*, *58*

shoulder pads 6, 44, *56*
silk 8, 10, 17
Simpson, Adele 20
Sinatra, Frank 25, *25*
skirts 6, 10, 14, *16*, *20*, 23, *25*, 28, 29, 38, 41, 52, 56, *56*, 57, *57*
snoods 6
Snow, Carmel 34, 39, 59
socks 49
spivs 17, 47
Stiebel, Victor 41
suits 10, *16*, 17, *36*, *43*, *44*, *46*, 47, 49, *52*
sweaters 12, *12*, *18*

trench coats 55
T-shirts 51, *51*

uniforms *6*, 36, 40, *40*, *42*, 48, 51
US Production Board 10, 31
Utility clothes *11*, *14*, 38, *40*, 41, *41*, *43*, 48, 52

vests 49
Vichy government 9, 32, 33

West, Vera 55
White, Walter 47
Women's Auxiliary Territorial Service 40
Women's Royal Air Force 40
Women's Royal Naval Service 40
Women's Voluntary Service 40
wool 10, *42*, 49, 50, *51*

zazous 47, *47*
zippers 10, 29
zoot-suiters 17, 44, *44*, 45, 47